Emma's Dead

Emma's Dead

Carol Malyon

To Janet
with love
Carol

Wolsak and Wynn . Toronto

Two sections of this book appeared in *Event*:
emma paces & paces
nurses chatter of weekends

Cover art and design: Rob Malyon
Author's photograph: Helen Humphreys
Typeset in Times Roman, printed in Canada by
The Coach House Press, Toronto.

The author wishes to acknowledge:
Rod Anderson   Mia Anderson
Kristin Andrychuk   Anne Archer
Martha Butterfield   James Deahl
Richard Harrison   Kim Maltman
Jeff Park   Martin Singleton

The Ontario Arts Council

The publishers gratefully acknowledge support by
The Canada Council and The Ontario Arts Council.

Wolsak and Wynn Publishers Ltd.
Don Mills Post Office Box 316
Don Mills, Ontario, Canada, M3C 2S7

Canadian Cataloguing in Publication Data
Malyon, Carol, 1933-
Emma's Dead
Poems.
ISBN O-919897-31-2

I. Title.
PS8576.A69E66 1992   C811'.54   C92-095792-7
PR9199.3.M36E66 1992

in memory of my father
& everyone i loved who died

emma was a ~~*figment of my imagination*~~ dream
~~*but even*~~ *the real ones were* ~~*figments*~~ also dreams

★

karen is a mother
she is a daughter
& tries to sort out which is which

she wonders:

is it possible to be a daughter
when a mother is lost forever?

she asks this over & over

gravestones ignore her

a small child tugs at her
& cries

momma?

momma?

★

o

no

o no

o

momma's dead

no

don't say that word

this must be a bad connection
phone me again

don't tell me dead

grant me an extra syllable

tell me:
i'm phoning about emma
she is better

dead?
my momma's dead?

but i've a little girl here
she's never even seen

she can't be dead

i still love her

★

o

emma falls down
her heart stops for a moment
her head cracks against
the hallway floor

a nurse drops her tray of pills
an aide comes running
all the patients stand & watch
emma practice to be dead

★

karen walks along the shore

the mist feels thick with a significance
she came here to escape

geese point toward her
then point away

tall oaks hurl acorns
against the sombre ground

joggers' feet are paddles
that pound the boardwalk rib-cage
try to change the beach's rhythm

karen ignores them

she watches a sea gull
painted on a post
it cries & cries

★

nurses have a game
they play reality
orientation

nurses tell emma:
it is thursday
it is raining
world events are taking place

but emma is in prison
people in uniform
force her to eat

they try to make her
play their game
want her to tell them her daughter's name

emma escapes them
she has forgotten she had a daughter

★

karen is crying
try not to listen

momma
don't pluck those little bits of memory
from your mind
don't fiddle with them
as they lie useless on your hand
don't save your breath & then let go

o no
they blow away

specks of dust
dance shiny for a moment
against a window

disappear
as a cloud takes over

★

emma almost remembers a child
blue thoughts unravel in her mind
she plucks at them & plucks
it is something to do

there used to be a child
a blue blanket was clutched tight
& then let go

emma almost feels that blanket
year after year
clutched by the child

that emma was fiercer
than grandparents & experts
if her child wanted a warm blue world
she could have one

emma wears a blue housecoat
she remembers a blanket
almost remembers a child

★

emma paces & paces nursing home corridors
hallways empty as her mind

as she erases herself
now her daughter
begins to blur around the edges
it is easy to see now
that parts of karen are missing

★

karen tries to remember twenty-three years
of words shared with her mother
in all that time
there must have been thousands
of words that would matter
only ten words a year
would still add up to two hundred & thirty
she cannot recall them

she retraces their walks
the sound of their footsteps crunching dry leaves
she studies the vacant pale smile of the sky

all the words she recalls are meals & tv shows & neighbours
& things that happened at work & happened at school

karen wants words that matter
ones which she can pass on to her own child

it is as though emma had told her:
there are only two copies of this message in the world
i have one
you have the other

her mother has lost one of the copies
perhaps karen's is only misplaced
perhaps when she no longer is weeping
she will find it packed in a carton or suitcase

karen believes this
she believes the copy is somewhere
she would give it to her daughter for safekeeping
if she could find it

karen fears
she & her daughter will walk inside silences
dry leaves will punctuate their empty conversations

always she will worry
there are words she ought to tell her daughter
but cannot recall them

perhaps her mother never had the words
to pass them on

there has been so much forgetting

★

emma finds a snapshot
in her bedside table drawer

a child plays on a beach

emma can see only outlines
without her glasses

she puts the snapshot
into someone else's drawer

perhaps it isn't theirs
it doesn't matter

she knows it isn't hers

★

hello momma

momma
this is karen
i've come back

momma
don't look away
this is karen
your little girl

unfold my memory out of moth-balls

don't leave it locked in dusty boxes
in rooms you won't return to

momma
stop folding wrinkles in your dress
& hug me back

★

there must be some mistake
where's my momma?

a straggled woman
who doesn't know me
sits on a chair beside her bed
she wears a plastic bracelet
printed with my momma's name

my momma's slim & stemmy
as a cattail down by the pond
she wears brown & willow-green
& soft shady colours

o look at this old woman
she is losing her clothes
she wears brown paper slippers
that have no shape

my daddy used to tell her
she had ballerina's feet
that should be dancing

he used to hold
both her little feet
inside one hand

i remember this
or else i dreamed it

o
these poor cold feet
let me warm them in my hands

★

there's nothing much to do
at sunny acres
emma walks the floor
she walks the floor all day

emma can't talk
to other patients
she's too forgetful
so are they

nurses talk at emma
their voices are cold as corridors
they say: how are we today?
let's take our pills

nurses remind her
to go to the bathroom
they remind each other
not to be angry
when it's too late

emma walks the hall
she remembers she had a husband
she had a child

she wonders what they looked like
& whether they had names

★

nurses chatter of weekends
new sheets are crisp on the beds
it is monday they tell her
monday emma
can you say it?

days used to have names
monday/washday
monday's child is fair of face

emma had a child one monday
emma's bottom scrubbed & shaved
& stained with antiseptic
doctors scoured her clean
of what had been crowding her insides
out popped a baby that needed a bath
emma knows it was harder at the time
but she is numb now
to even her new pains

emma had a child one monday
she remembers the name of the day
the child's name takes longer

monday back to school
monday back to work
patterns that could be handled
one piece at a time

it is monday
new sheets are crisp on the beds
before the old ones are even wet

there'll be a singsong after lunch
come on ladies
let's sing the monday song:
monday
fun day

★

karen talks a lot to doctors
long-distance

she wants her child
to have a grandmother
she wants her mother
to have a grandchild
she thinks a grandchild
could make her mother better

emma doesn't even know
karen has a child
karen cries about this
in the middle of the night

karen talks to the doctors
about a transfer to her town

emma doesn't care
emma's already there
or somewhere

★

emma looks too young to be admitted
to sunny acres
her body's aging slower than her mind

she still looks fresh & neat
visitors try to talk to her
they think she's one of them

emma thinks they might be right
& tries leaving when they do
she knows she doesn't belong

but soon emma looks like everyone else

her clothes get mixed up in the laundry
nothing fits
her hem hangs down
her stockings sag toward her slippers

her glasses fall off the bedside table
they break & are never replaced

emma keeps her head down
to hide her empty eyes

visitors avoid her
emma avoids everyone

★

karen is making mrs thompson's
chocolate macaroons
they are dark & sweet & textured
with memories of childhood

karen stirs around some corner of her mind

a child walks up the street beside her mother
toward mrs thompson's house
then plays on a verandah
enamel-hot with summer
coco-matting bristles
imprint a prickled pattern
on her bare legs

emma & mrs thompson
clink teacups against saucers
karen listens what the world is
fitting jigsaw puzzle pieces into place

war & church & knitting
& husbands who collect
insurance payments door-to-door
to earn a living

life is solid as a dream
a child wakes up one day
to find she's lost a father
& hardly had one

so what is father?
a father is like
mrs thompson's husband
fathers wear scratchy
cigarette-smoke clothes
fathers talk in English accents
fathers forget to close the bathroom door
when they are peeing
fathers' wives talk louder
when this happens

fathers know how to drive a car
mrs thompson's husband
can tuck his family inside
a tiny austin car
like his pocket

mrs thompson's like emma
mrs thompson's not the same
she mails out christmas presents
in the summer
her kitchen smells like chutney
there is clutter everywhere

inside a kitchen cupboard
the thompsons keep a tree trunk
it is alive
the house is built around it
above the ordinary roof
branches burst in green

this seems no more amazing
than chocolate macaroons
& all the other magic
of their lives

★

what is happening here?

why does she do this?

emma walks along this corridor
as though she lives here

emma
this is no place for you
you still are beautiful
you've got some sense left

emma
don't stay

★

dear momma
is everything all right?
why don't you write?

dear momma
what's the matter?
your last letter was almost
an empty piece of paper
you wrote dear
& then stopped half-way through my name

★

emma is lost again
like little bo peep
or someone she read stories about
when karen was a child
& emma was a mother
who still remembered
where she lived

hansel & gretel are lost
emma can't find them
their forest looks like a city
gingerbread houses are made of bricks

tell me a story says karen

or she used to when she was little
& was somewhere
emma could find her

karen learned to read
& moved away

★

karen & her toddler
walk beside the sea

they build castles in the sand
& pretend they'll last forever

they listen to voices inside sea shells

emma is far away
a kite string tugs at karen
as she stretches against the sky

★

emma tries to pay attention
to what people say
but their voices are far away

her thinking trips over itself
& has trouble getting untangled

by the time it does the talk has always
turned to something else

emma learns to look
as though she understands
she smiles a lot & nods
she says really!
& no kidding!
& hopes that she makes sense

emma didn't have to be a file clerk
or a teacher or a nurse
she could have been an actress
she has talent

★

karen's baby plays on a beach
she has a pail & shovel
& sand that waits for her to move it

karen watches her
& remembers a snapshot in emma's album
that looked like this

she thinks:
emma could look at that snapshot
& see her grandchild
if she knew she had a grandchild

emma looks at a snapshot
of a baby on a beach

she pretends that karen
is still that little child

★

emma turns into an old woman
she considers a blue rinse
spots darken on her skin
lumps thicken inside it
each time she dares to face the mirror
her body betrays her a little more
she doesn't recognize the stranger
that stares back

emma turns into an old woman
she regrets never learning to play bridge

emma turns into her mother
they will put her in sunny acres
she will have to hide in corners & mumble to herself
to block the others out
they won't realize she needs privacy
in order to survive

emma could be fifty or seventy-five
it doesn't matter
her genes had always known
she would turn into an old woman
at this moment

other women who are her age
have already turned into their mothers

★

karen has pale shoulders
& a lover
who runs his tongue
along her shoulders slowly
any time she likes

karen has pale shoulders
& a lover & a baby

perhaps that's all she needs

★

emma's world shrinks & holds her tight:
a house
a room
a bed

she pulls blankets around her
hides inside them

if she were a fetus now
she would choose not to be born

but how wildly once this woman
wanted to get out
how she smashed stretched pushed
bashed ripped hammered
out of her mother's belly

how badly she must have wanted air
to fight so hard

★

dear momma
i've found a job/i've lost it

but i can't come home
this christmas/this summer/this christmas

dear momma
don't worry
everything's all right

★

emma shaves her legs for henry
but won't let him touch them

he says he loves her
emma doesn't believe him

she is turning into an old woman
so she has to make him go

her cat yowls
& rubs against her
always wanting to be fed

years stretch empty
white & sterile as a bed

empty is the only way
emma dares to choose

★

a log floats on the bay
only birds & fish
can read its totem symbols

karen is changing here

perfectly still now
she feels it happen

her belly swells
pulls the rest of her
tightly around it

deep inside her
her child hums
a small strong song

cormorants ride the waves
like searching periscopes

a blue heron ignores her

gulls swirl perpetual question marks
against the endless sky

some old woman walks the shore
karen ignores her

only sea gulls cry

★

emma likes to go to movies
with a man
likes holding hands

emma likes it when henry hugs her
she likes to hug him back

for anything else
emma's going to need a lot of time

★

karen whispers her secret
to the wind

listen momma
there is something i can't tell you
trees keep whispering
your soft name

momma
how could i tell you

inside my belly
a child is humming
is calling to me
with your name

momma

momma

*

emma meets a man
this surprises her
she hasn't been looking
but he has
since his wife died

henry's been hunting
someone to sew on buttons
clean out cupboards
share his bed

★

dear momma
i am fine
love karen

dear momma
i like vancouver

★

emma walks along a street
her footsteps are careful & precise
her pain is invisible

a child kicked inside her belly
twenty years ago
she still struggles
to let that infant go

★

train wheels click faster than karen's heartbeat
fast as the heartbeat of a fetus
that flickers inside her

a child smaller than the thumb
of a hand against her throat

each stop along the track
demands a new decision

the train whistles against the night
like a youngster in a graveyard

★

karen had a childhood
it was like the apartment
she lives in

rooms are snug & comfortable
walls are perfect for handball
corridors are dark cool caves
the basement is dark & scary
she avoids it

on the roof
she is taller than trees & houses
she sees everything
but is invisible

one day in the hallway
someone she knows is glad to see her
he hugs her tight
his body is strong & hard
& uncomfortable
his mouth is ugly

he hurts & hurts her
until she promises
she won't tell

karen lives in an apartment
it is not like a childhood
childhood is over

★

karen has two snapshots of her father:

a man beside a sailboat
lies buried in a jewelry box
in seventeen pieces

upon her dresser
a man wears a business suit
he is a stereotype of the word father:
leaves in the morning
returns when a small child goes off to bed

o silly crisp white shirt
collar tight around his neck
tie choking it in place

o stupid leather belt
pretending it knows everything
(karen thinks it once lashed out at her
for some small mistake)

o pretentious three-piece pinstripe suit
& polished shoes

o absurd person
to wear a face that is ambiguous
a suit so pompous & ridiculous

karen thinks she can remember
a fishnet sweater father
in baggy pants & old scuffed shoes
who whistled bird songs
as she rode upon his shoulders
but she has no snapshot for confirmation

she thinks that person
drew sketches in her scribbler
but no longer has the scribbler
& can't be sure

this is the tyranny of snapshots

karen does not like this pinstripe man
does not want him to be her father
but dares not throw the photo out
it is someone to touch
& be sure of

★

karen's grandmother calls karen
her favourite grandchild
she always says this

karen has always needed
to be a favourite

the words are soft as marshmallow
warm as hot chocolate inside her

at the funeral
karen searches the room in vain
for other grandchildren who were not favourites

it is too late now
for her grandmother to explain

★

after school
karen cooks supper
& pretends grandmother cooks it

she pretends
grandmother remembers
to put water in the kettle
& unplug it when it boils

grandmother pretends
karen only sets the table

emma comes home from work
& seems to believe them

they all pretend that grandmother
stays inside when it is cold
puts on a coat over her nightgown
& boots over her slippers
still remembers her way back home
won't get pneumonia
will have the strength to recover

pretending is harder than it looks

★

there are too many women in this house

karen walks carefully
between her mother & grandmother

she concentrates on her footsteps
afraid that she will fall
they will measure
whether she fell closer
to her mother or grandmother

they never allow her to travel
a distance too far to measure

★

karen's grandmother stands
against a window
holds fine bone china to the sun

karen sees light
through the saucer
sees fingers moving behind it

she sees her grandmother
against the window
sunlight shines through her

karen holds her gently
afraid to break

★

emma dreams

people pull off little pieces
of her skin
they don't notice she is bleeding
she distracts them
so they won't be upset by seeing blood

she dreams

her skin is gone
her blood & guts & muscle
glisten in the sun

dreams

she walks along the street
& meets all the people she tried to please
they have pieces of her skin
stored in dresser drawers & cupboards
when they look away & retch
emma grabs them & starts to scream:
remember me   i'm emma
this is what was left when
you tore my skin away

she has these nightmares every night
in the morning she is tired

emma's always tired

★

karen's grandmother feeds her
she feeds her anything
that karen wants

she serves eggs boiled or poached or scrambled
she will even make an omelette
or french toast

karen is in the centre
of a fragile eggshell world

★

karen loves her grandmother
she loves her best
it's a secret
only karen knows
& her mother & her grandmother

but emma remembers having a grandmother
now she is waiting to be one

karen is only twelve years old
emma will have to wait a while

★

emma wants to be the mother
it isn't easy
she wants her mother to be the grandmother

grandmothers have it nice
they don't do anything
but love the child

emma's mother saves all the problems
until emma comes home from work

emma reads about this kind of family
in women's magazines:
the mothers save the problems for the fathers

emma had never wanted
to be a father

★

karen grows up
her grandmother watches her

it is amazing
she has never watched a child grow up before

karen grows up
but her grandmother gets to watch

★

emma teaches school

these were the choices:
bank teller
teacher
secretary
nurse

she didn't want to be a teacher
but the other things seemed worse

she spends all day
with other people's children

other teachers
spend all day with karen

sometimes emma thinks this is funny
but not too often

★

karen sits on a rock beside a lake
she is thinking of sailboats

the rock & the water
have been waiting here forever

karen touches the morning
morning tastes brown & green & sweet
the rock is solid beneath her

her toes visit the world
they trace clam tracks along the corrugated sand
they swim with minnows

beyond her
boats & men & poles
are silent shadows inside the mist

a man pulls a fish out of the water
its body flaps against the sky
it strangles inside the alien air

karen screams
she startles the fisherman
he drops the fish

karen screams & screams & screams
boats glide toward grey space
the fishermen let her do this
because she's little

★

emma moves back in with her mother
it is awful but she can stand it
she has karen to keep her going

emma grows stronger
her mother gets weaker

emma has won at something
she's not sure what

★

a man stands beside a sailboat
he is black & white & shiny
on a polished hall table

it is not possible to understand
a boat can be broken
that a father floats in cold water
forever

karen rips the snapshot
into seventeen pieces

then saves them

★

emma's husband dies
it's just as well
she can't stand being happy
too much longer
she knows she doesn't deserve it

when they call to tell her
she collapses with relief

she'd known it couldn't last
he'd soon have noticed
other women wore polish on their nails
fixed fancy foods for supper
didn't let their babies cry or drool or get the croup
emma couldn't have stood the competition
of all those perfect women too much longer

she'd tried not to look at him too often
in case it was bad luck

at the funeral parlour
emma keeps a piece of onion in a kleenex
in case she needs to cry

★

karen has a father
he can draw anything

karen knows this
although he only draws sailboats

he draws them everywhere
on newspaper edges   on paper serviettes
they take up whole pages
in karen's scribbler

karen waits
one day he will draw one so large
he & karen can climb aboard
& find an ocean

instead he draws one
climbs inside
sails away

★

donny has a picture in his pocket

emma is beautiful
her face is almost serene

she balances between karen
who almost is able to stand still
& her mother
who still is able to walk

they hold hands

emma holds karen tightly
emma's mother holds tight to emma

★

karen has a childhood

days are flitting as mayflies
& endless as sky

days break up when they happen
& blow away

karen chases after
gathers small bits inside
her butterfly-net mind

karen watches a flower grow

karen
& her mother
& her father
& ladybugs & bumblebees
that scratch their wings against the lazy sky

karen watches a flower
she thinks she can watch it forever

this is karen's world
she still trusts it

★

emma croons lullabies to karen
she soothes her baby with sadness

they rock together
& wait for something bad to happen

★

emma & her baby rock to & fro
her mother is visiting & telling
the persian carpet story:

we saw this carpet at a farm sale
when we unrolled it to have a look
you threw up right in the middle
we had to buy it

emma has heard this tale so often
she feels like throwing up again

she thinks it must have been something
like morning sickness:
eight years old & pregnant
with imaginary families

they threw out her teddy bear
& brought home a baby sister
she played with marbles instead

emma was almost invisible
playing on that carpet under the table
she softened the rug's geometry with people

she made families of marbles
small ones were children
large ones were parents grandparents
aunts & uncles

all the green ones lived together
in a green pattern on the carpet
this was supposed to be their home
a blue family lived in a blue section
a red family in a red section
& so on

the ones left over were old maids

patterns were everywhere
waiting to be schools & stores & playgrounds
lines joined them up like roads
for children to skip along & hopscotch
& step on cracks

emma thinks the child she used to be
was almost crazy

she rocks harder to comfort her baby
& that child

★

emma names her baby karen
she picks that name
because her mother hates it

she knows she's foolish
& thinks it's lucky
she likes the name herself

if she didn't
she would use it anyway

★

emma has a husband

donny's blonde where she is dark
straight where she is round
hard where she is soft

he speaks loving words
that vibrate everywhere inside her
she's so happy she can't stand it

donny almost belongs to her
he's so perfect
emma knows she'd better get a baby quick
before he goes

it takes a lot of loving
to make a perfect baby
emma's always scared
scared she can't grow one
or that he'll get tired of her
before they get one started

she can
he doesn't
but emma's still always scared

★

emma goes on dates to please her mother

she makes up details
that her mother will enjoy

★

emma grows up

she is pretty good at everything:
schoolwork
homework
working after school
helping around the house

this doesn't leave
much time for dating
it's just as well

at the high school dances
emma stays in the ladies' room
until she can go home

*

emma washes the dishes
her mother tells her
the wilsons are dead
killed in a car crash

emma cries

the wilsons lived down the street
emma pretended they were her parents
she went there straight from school
they gave her milk & graham wafers
& let her play with their baby

each time emma returned
her mother was angry & silent
that silence could make emma do anything
she stopped going to the wilsons
her mother was still angry & silent
but emma didn't feel as guilty

she cries harder
all those visits that she missed
wash down the drain

★

emma has an urge or itch or something
she is only fourteen years old
& doesn't know what to call it
when she is older she still won't know

thoughts almost happen inside her mind
until she stops them

her body tries to unfasten
tissue restricts it

sometimes it happens
as she walks along the street
it's hard to walk so she walks faster
no one must know

emma invents masturbation
it doesn't help
she uninvents it

★

emma's grade eight picture
is being taken inside the classroom
there's no use pretending any longer
that school days are a playground
no one believes it

emma pretends to be pretty
a black satin hairband smooths her shiny hair
she wears a draw-string blouse
a dark cardigan on top
hides her empty chest

later when it's not empty
she will have to wear a cardigan
to hide that

emma sits at the back of the room
the teacher trusts her
the boy she likes sits farther forward

when emma meets him on the street
she acts as though she doesn't see him
but she watches him in school
if she sits just right
she can gaze at his profile

the boy watches the camera
emma watches him
but pretends to watch the camera

this is the last class picture
they won't be taken in high school
if emma wants to remember high school
she can get another copy of grade eight

★

for the grade six picture
all the little kids are being posed
cross-legged on the ground

emma is not supposed
to sit down on the ground
in case her bottom catches cold
her mother won't like this picture

emma is ugly
her part is crooked
elastics pull her straggled hair
toward her ears

she wears bloomers
& thick cotton stockings
she bulges like a flour sack
her grandmother knitted her ugly sweater
her mother sewed her ugly skirt
emma pretends that she likes them

grade six is hard
emma goes to church each sunday
& knows that hard & ugly shouldn't matter
she is beautiful inside
she tries to believe this

emma sits cross-legged on the ground
her skirt covers her knees
her hands hold each other
& keep her skirt in place

she is nervous
a boy sits cross-legged beside her
he is sitting so close
his knee rests on top of hers

her mother told her never to sit cross-legged
maybe this is why

★

emma bounces a ball against a wall
she bounces it each day

ordinary is easy
she could bounce ordinary forever

but there is a ritual she must go through

not move or laugh or talk is harder
but she needs these for church & school
she'll find other uses later

emma uses one hand & then another
until she can juggle

she hops on one foot & then the other
this is almost as tiring as high heels
almost as ridiculous

emma spins her arms away
she spins them back
this is silly
but lots of things are silly

she curtsies & salutes until it's easy

& away she goes
emma spins around

one day she will spin into a woman
when the time comes she will be ready

*

for her grade four picture
emma acts all grown up

she has a baby sister
so she might as well grow up

emma's dress is pretty
snow white & seven dwarfs
dance everywhere in circles holding hands
like children playing in a schoolyard

emma's saddle shoes
mark time until prince charming

★

for her grade two picture
emma tries to look
cute as a kewpie doll
a huge white bow is fastened
to her birthday-present hair

she holds her hands together
so many things are wrong to do
if she holds them tight
perhaps her mother & the teacher
& the other kids
will think she's perfect
maybe they'll like her

if emma had fingernails
they would dig into her hands

she tilts her head to one side
tries to look like she is good

★

emma's father comes & goes

sometimes he is tall
& sometimes short

he has one name & then another

emma learns to call him
uncle

★

emma has a teddy bear
& a father
& a mother
in order of importance

anyway
emma's teddy bear is softer
than her bony mother

★

emma's mother is not unkind

sometimes
she pats emma on the head

sometimes
she has the urge to hug her
but refrains

emma's mother
doesn't want to be effusive

★

emma's mother falls downstairs
nothing happens

she brews tea leaves
from a lady down the street
& throws up for a week

finally she finds a man with instruments
but he's too scared
he says she should have come
two months sooner

at last she knows she has to keep it
& hopes at least it'll be a boy

after emma's born
her mother won't hold her or look at her
until she has to take her home

she remembers the pain
to tell emma about it later

Emma's Dead is Carol Malyon's second book of poetry. Reversing the order of the narrative, the poet traces the progress of Alzheimer disease, beginning with the final stage, and working back to the patient's healthy self, leaving the reader with a potent portrait of the person Emma used to be, as well as the woman she became.

About *Headstand*:

"... elegant, spare writing."
— *Canadian Book Review Annual*

"... the humour and unforced flow of the conversational pieces make them ... engaging and .. thought-provoking."
— *Books in Canada*

Wolsak and Wynn